LIVING IN HARSH ENVIRONMENTS

Written by Mary-Anne Creasy

Flying Start
to Literacy®

Contents

Introduction   4

     Surviving extreme cold   6

     Surviving extreme heat   8

Chapter 1: Extreme cold   10

     The Arctic: Living traditionally   11

     Yakutsk, Russia: Living today   14

Chapter 2: Extreme heat   20

     The Danakil Desert, Ethiopia:
     Living traditionally   22

     Dubai, UAE: Living today   26

Conclusion   30

Index   32

Introduction

Have you ever been outside on a chilly day and felt yourself shivering and your teeth chattering? This is your body's defence mechanism against extremely cold temperatures. It helps keep your body warm.

And on really hot days, when you find yourself covered in sweat, this is your body's defence against extremely hot temperatures. Sweat on your skin helps you stay cool.

The human body is extraordinary. Like all mammals, humans can maintain their core body temperature at around 37 degrees Celsius, in both freezing winters and hot summers. If our body temperature falls below 34 degrees Celsius or rises over 40 degrees Celsius, the consequences can be fatal.

People who live in extreme climates have to maintain their core body temperature to survive.

Surviving extreme cold

People who live in or visit extremely cold places must take precautions to survive. If they lose too much body heat, their core body temperature drops. When this happens, the person's life is at risk.

People have been able to live in these extremely cold places for thousands of years. They have done so by building appropriate housing and wearing the right clothing when they venture outdoors. Today, modern technology allows people to live more comfortably in the harsh climate.

In cold weather, thick clothing works like insulation. It traps body heat close to your body and stops it from escaping.

During a snowstorm, the temperature can drop rapidly.

The cold can be dangerous if proper care is not taken:

❄ At –55 degrees Cesius, the moisture in your nostrils freezes, and the cold air makes it difficult to breathe.

❄ At –70 degrees Celsius, exposed skin becomes numb and you can get frostbite.

❄ When the temperature drops below –80 degrees Celsius, after five to ten minutes, fingers and toes begin to ache, the air stings your face and you begin to feel tired. At this temperature, people should not wear metal glasses. If they take them off, the metal will stick to the skin and can rip it off.

Surviving extreme heat

In extremely hot climates, our bodies try to lose body heat. If they cannot do this, our bodies overheat and our lives are at risk.

People who live in or visit these extremely hot climates need to be prepared. Amazingly, people have lived in extreme heat environments for thousands of years. They have been able to do this by living in appropriate shelters, adjusting their diet and wearing the right clothing. Modern technology makes it possible for more people to live in hot, dry desert environments.

In hot weather, you can easily overheat your body when playing sport. Drink plenty of fluids and rest when you start to heat up.

Many cities in the world have heat waves during summer. But heat waves don't last more than a few weeks at the most. It is an extreme weather pattern and not part of the permanent climate.

Heat can be dangerous if proper care is not taken:

- We sweat to cool our bodies, but if the sweat runs out because we have not replaced the fluid our bodies overheat.

- When our bodies become too hot, it affects our brains and leads to confusion and unconsciousness, known as heatstroke.

- Other serious symptoms of heatstroke are cramping muscles and dry skin.

Chapter 1

Extreme cold

The survival of people who live in extremely cold climates depends on two things – their ability to reduce heat loss and to increase heat production.

Today, technology helps people to live in extremely cold environments. But what about in the past, when technology such as lights and heaters were not available?

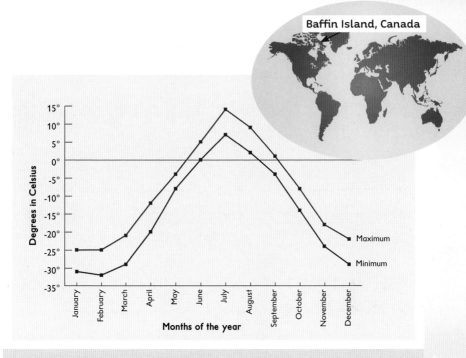

The annual temperatures in Baffin Island, Canada

The Arctic: Living traditionally

For thousands of years, the indigenous peoples of the Arctic region spent the winter months living and hunting on the expanded ice. They lived in this freezing environment because food was plentiful, and they learnt how to adapt to the conditions.

These Arctic dwellers lived for months at a time like this, surviving without heating, electricity or modern building materials. They adapted to their environment by sourcing everything they used, wore and ate from the materials around them.

Food, clothing and transportation

Indigenous peoples of the Arctic ate mainly fish, whale and seal. They burned seal blubber for heat to cook and for warmth, and also to provide light. They wore two layers of caribou skin and fur, sewing the skins together using needles made from animal bones. On their feet, they wore boots made from seal skin.

They used sleds for transportation, which were made of wood, animal bones or baleen from a whale's mouth. Dogs pulled the sleds over the snow and ice.

In preparation for winter, salmon were hung out to dry in the summer months.

In some parts of the Arctic, people used reindeer to pull sleds.

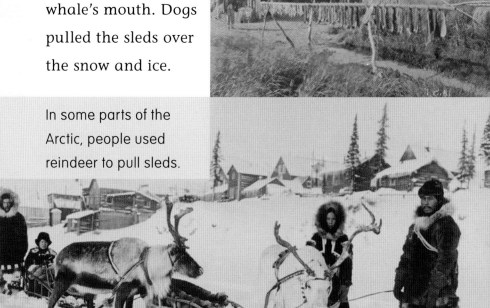

Inuit constructing an igloo, 1924

Igloos

The Inuit of Canada and Greenland used snow to build temporary homes in winter called igloos. Snow is an excellent insulating material because of the air trapped inside. Blocks of hard, compressed snow were cut and stacked into a dome shape that could shelter up to 20 people. People slept on platforms of ice covered in furs. Outside, it could be –75 degrees Celsius, but inside, with body warmth, the temperature could reach up to 20 degrees Celsius.

Yakutsk, Russia: Living today

The coldest city on Earth is Yakutsk, in eastern Russia. Here, the average maximum temperature during January is –75 degrees Celsius. Yakutsk has one of the biggest ranges of extreme temperatures in the world – nearly 100 degrees between the summer and winter temperatures. Yakutsk is cold because it is very far north, just 450 kilometres south of the Arctic Circle.

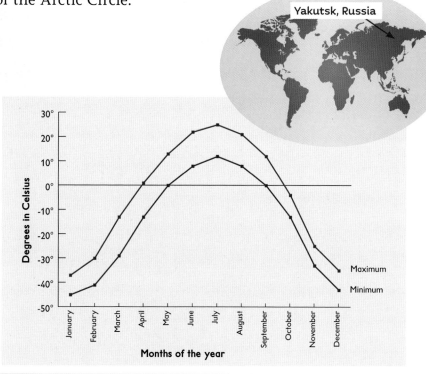

The annual temperatures in Yakutsk, Russia

Yakutsk locals say wearing fur is the only way to beat the cold.

Going outside

For someone who is not used to the Yakutsk winter, or who does not have the correct clothing, the cold air can make their body go into shock and extreme pain, even after only ten minutes outside. During the coldest part of the year, most people never go outside, unless it is absolutely necessary.

Babies and young children do not go outside during the winter. Their bodies are smaller and would not stay warm. When the temperature drops to dangerous levels, younger children can stay home from school. If they need to go somewhere, people take a taxi.

Going to school

When children go to school, it takes them about 30 minutes to get dressed with the many layers of clothes they need to wear before they go outside. They must wear two layers of pants – a thick outer layer for outside, and another pair to wear indoors. Many people wear a scarf over their faces, a woollen or fur hat, and a hood. Two pairs of thick socks are essential, and some children wear mittens over the top of a thinner pair of gloves so they can use their fingers.

To get to school, most children will catch a bus or walk if it's close. Driving on icy, snowy roads when the air is thick with fog can be dangerous.

These children are walking to school on a typical winter's day in Yakutsk. It is −65° C.

In Yakutsk, January is the coldest month.

Cars, planes and phones

Machines are affected by the cold. Cars must be left with the engine running. If you turn off the engine, it might not start again because the fluids in the engine could freeze.

If you want to go to Yakutsk in winter, you need to fly there, but only in a plane that can operate in temperatures below –75 degrees Celsius. Cameras freeze up within ten minutes in the cold air and even get a layer of frost on them. Phones use more battery power in the cold and need to be warmed frequently or they freeze up, too.

Food

Because of the cold, crops cannot grow easily in Yakutsk. People mainly eat meat and lots of fish. Almost everything else must be brought in from other places. Yakutsk is a very isolated city that is many kilometres from other towns and cities in Russia.

An outdoor market in Yakutsk, where people buy frozen fish and other meat.

A house covered in snow and ice in the world's coldest city.

Summer in Yakutsk

Despite this extreme cold, locals prefer it to the brief summers where temperatures reach above 27 degrees Celsius and the air becomes thick with mosquitoes. The buildings are not air-conditioned so the heat is unbearable.

During the brief summer, people rush to repair buildings and check heating systems to prepare for the next winter when the extreme cold once more grips the city.

Chapter 2

Extreme heat

There are many places in the world that have extreme heat
almost all year around. This extreme climate requires
humans to adapt in both simple and extraordinary ways.
Today, people also use modern technology to change
their environment so they don't have to adapt.

There are deserts on every continent. They can be hot like the Sahara Desert in Africa or cold like the polar desert of Antarctica.

The hottest, driest places in the world are deserts. They are extremely harsh environments to live in, with temperatures in some deserts soaring above 50 degrees Celsius during the day, then often dropping to below freezing (0 degrees Celsius) at night.

But people have survived in deserts for thousands of years, using shelters made of cloth or sticks, without electrical heating, air-conditioning or running water.

Others however, have used modern technology to change their living environments to make them cool and comfortable all year around.

The Danakil Desert, Ethiopia: Living traditionally

The hottest climate in the world is the Danakil Desert, Ethiopia in Eastern Africa. It often reaches 50 degrees Celsius during the day. Unlike many hot deserts, however, the temperature does not get cold at night – even winter nights can be 30 degrees Celsius. This is because much of the land is more than 90 metres below sea level and is sinking even lower.

Not much grows in this burning hot desert, and water is scarce. Often a hot wind blows, which can cause sandstorms. Yet, despite all these harsh conditions, people still live here.

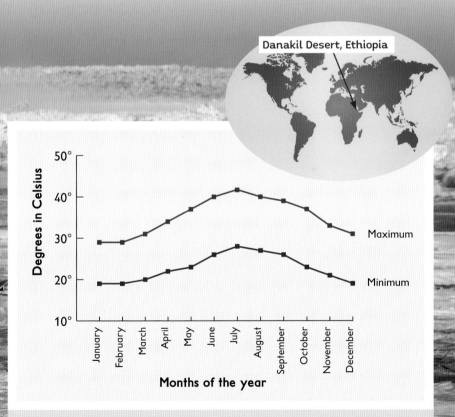

Danakil Desert, Ethiopia

The annual temperatures in the Danakil Desert, Ethiopia

The Afar people

The Afar people live in the Danakil Desert. They have mined the vast deposits of valuable salt found in this desert for thousands of years. The Afar people live in small communities with their livestock. They are nomads. They herd their animals around to forage, or travel with them to find new grazing. They live in shelters made from sticks and woven palm leaves that their camels carry on their backs when they move.

These Afar women are collecting water from a well. They often have to walk for hours to reach a source of water.

These Afar people have filled their containers with water and are returning to their village.

The food they eat comes mainly from their animals. Goat meat and milk make up most of their diet. They also eat bread and porridge, made from flour, water and butter, which they prepare with goats' milk. For the Afar, their animals are their most valuable possession. They will often use them for trading to get flour, spices and other things they cannot get from the desert.

Water is essential in this extreme heat, and the Afar know where hidden water wells are, and how to dig for water if the wells are dry. They have passed this knowledge down from one generation to the next and it has helped them to survive in one of the harshest climates in the world.

Dubai, UAE: Living today

Today, Dubai in the United Arab Emirates is a modern, gleaming city of skyscrapers. But once it was a small fishing village on the Arabian Peninsula.

For thousands of years, people on the Arabian Peninsula either lived in small villages in mud huts, or as nomads who moved where their animals could forage for food and water. They lived in tents, which protected them from burning sun, intense cold and sandstorms.

Today, some countries in Arabia are extremely wealthy because of the huge oil deposits under the land. Their simple nomadic existence is now far behind them. They have built cities on top of the burning sand dunes, with comfortable air-conditioned buildings to protect their inhabitants from the ferocious heat.

Dubai is such a city. It has some of the biggest shopping malls and hotels in the world. Many are linked by enclosed air-conditioned walkways, so people never have to emerge to face the extreme heat.

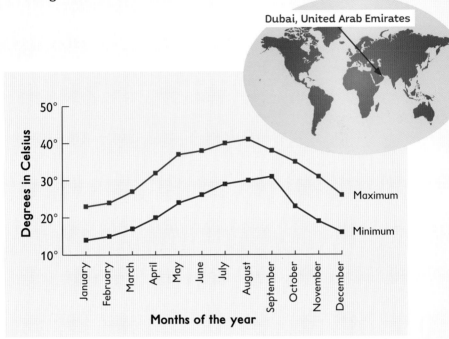

Dubai, United Arab Emirates

In Dubai, winter is mild and pleasant. However, between May and August the temperature often reaches 40° C and does not drop below 30° C at night.

During summer, many people spend all day inside these malls, which don't just have shops, but serve as air-conditioned leisure centres. They have restaurants, entertainment and activities. One mall has a winter theme park with a ski slope. Another has an ice-skating rink and an aquarium tunnel.

This indoor ski slope is in Dubai, where the outdoor temperature is often more than 40°C during the day in summer.

If you do need to go outside to catch a bus, there are air-conditioned bus shelters. The city is planning air-conditioned walkways, which would operate during summer.

The city of Dubai was built in a desert.

To keep the growing number of visitors and citizens cooler and more comfortable, Dubai intends to build a temperature-controlled city. The project will include hospitals, cinemas and apartments that are connected by glass-enclosed walkways and streets, and even a tram network.

Adapting to the extreme heat is not encouraged in this desert city, where many people complain that the temperatures inside are cold enough to wear a jacket.

Conclusion

People prefer to live in climates where they do not have to suffer the discomfort of extreme cold or heat. Although some people have adapted to harsh climates over thousands of years, most people today use modern technology to make their environments more comfortable.

Index

Arctic 11, 12, 14

clothing 12, 16

cold climates 10, 14-19

core body temperature 5, 6

Danakil Desert 22-25

deserts 8, 21, 22-25, 29

Dubai 26-29

food 12, 18, 25, 26, 28

heatwaves 8

hot climates 8, 20-29

igloos 13

nomads 24, 26

transport 12, 16, 17, 28

water 25, 26

Yakutsk 14-19